Introd[...]

Welshpool is a busy market [...] century. It was described in [...] and the appearance of opulence i[...] [...] throughout the place, perhaps owing to its trade in Welsh flannels, which is carried on here to a very great extent. The corner stones whereon its prosperity is founded are the flannel trade and the canal'. Offa's Dyke Path, Glyndŵr's Way and The Severn Valley Way all run through this area, and sections of each are visited on these walks.

The routes described in this book range from 1½ to 8 miles and all follow rights of way or permissive paths. Some are easy-going walks while others are more demanding, though none are mountainous. The majority can be undertaken by those accompanied by children – if you are with younger ones, **Walks 1** and **7** are especially suitable. Many of the walks have summit views and a good proportion include gentler routes along rivers or the Montgomery Canal, sometimes both. Woodland also features in a number of the walks, and there are often refreshment stops.

Some of the routes can be linked to make longer walks. All of them have been given fairly generous times for completion, so energetic walkers will be able to shorten these durations, whereas those who love to linger, or with young families, may need to add extra time. Most of the walks cross farmland, so you must always keep your dog on a lead.

The Tourist Information Centre, by the main car park, is very useful if you want to know more about the region, and a weather forecast can be obtained at www.met-office.gov.uk or by ringing 09003 444 900 (charge). Market day in Welshpool is Monday.

Thanks are extended to the Rights of Way Office in Llandrindrod Wells, and in particular Mark Chapman, for all the friendly help and advice we received.

Enjoy your walking!

WALK 1
LLANFAIR CAEREINION

DESCRIPTION This walk makes a great day out for anyone, particularly if accompanied by children. The journey, starting at Welshpool and going to and from Llanfair Caereinion, is by the Welshpool and Llanfair Light Railway, a treat in itself. The walk takes you through Llanfair, now a small and quiet town, but with a long history as a busy stopping place for stagecoaches travelling between Aberystwyth and Shrewsbury. The architecture is varied and interesting, making it a very attractive place to visit. Deri Wood is small and on a fairly steep slope next to the River Banwy, but it has been imaginatively laid out, with plenty of benches and picnic areas. Many of the tree species are also labelled. There are plenty of choices for a lunch stop, whether for a picnic, fish and chips, a pub or café meal. Allow 2 hours for the actual walk of around 2½ miles, plus the rail journey and any stops for lunch, shopping etc, in town. So take it easy and enjoy this day.

START From Welshpool take a train on the Welshpool & Llanfair Light Railway (station Grid Ref: SJ 216075). The walk starts at Llanfair Railway Station, Grid Ref: SJ 106068.

DIRECTIONS From Welshpool centre, go along the A458 out of town until you reach the roundabout, where it meets the A490. The Light Railway station is easily visible just off the roundabout. There is ample parking (it is just a five or ten minute walk up from the centre of Welshpool). A board shows departure times, or you can obtain a timetable from the station or from the Tourist Information Centre in Welshpool.

Take the train from Welshpool and enjoy the lovely and tranquil scenery, as the train puffs its way to Llanfair. The railway was opened in 1903, after years of failed attempts to raise enough money for the construction of the line. It ran only until 1931 as a combined passenger and goods service, when the passenger service was dropped. In 1956 the doomed railway was taken over by enthusiasts, all volunteers, and from then until the present the line and facilities have been steadily improved and upgraded. There is a station café at each end of the journey.

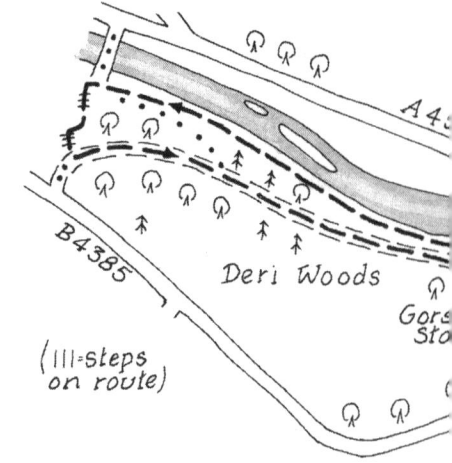

1 At Llanfair Caereinion, cross the River Banwy just outside the station, using the beautifully crafted suspension footbridge. It's a fine example of the technology so often used to construct metal bridges, but here built throughout in wood. On the other side, follow the path by the river, turning left on reaching the houses and then right, heading towards the town. There is a signpost part way along, so follow the direction for 'Riverside Walk'. Turn right at the T-junction and walk down to the main road. Cross straight over. A path by the side of the large building (The Institute), will take you to the church of St Mary.

2 There is a sign in the churchyard directing you to Fynnon Fair (St Mary's) Well. It's worth visiting, as it's a pre-Christian Holy Well and was a place of pilgrimage and healing. The church itself has some nice stained glass windows. From the front of the church, look for Samuel Roberts' Sundial (he was a famous local clockmaker) and then go up to the road and turn right. A short distance along on the right is an information board

WALK 1

and a footpath. This is the start of the walk through Deri Woods.

3 Go down the steps and, where the path diverges, take the right fork. It will take you straight down to the river. The walk through the woods is pleasant and easy. About halfway along is the old Pump House. Carry on until you come to a long footbridge across the river. Go past this and straightaway the path veers left and upwards. Take the left turn to continue back through the woods at a higher level.

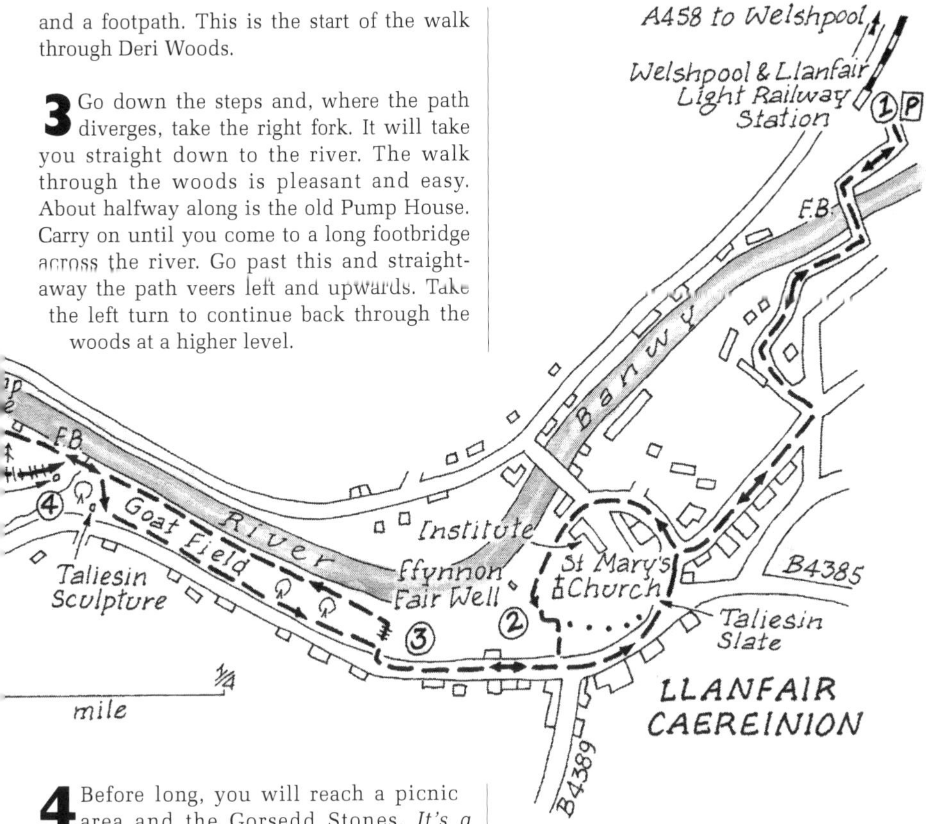

4 Before long, you will reach a picnic area and the Gorsedd Stones. *It's a mock stone circle and looks wonderfully atmospheric, standing in this leafy woodland clearing. There is also a marvellous tree root sculpture, made into a seat. If you look carefully you will see a face carved into it, resembling a Toby Jug.* Take the path down to the river, cross the bridge over the side stream and go up the steps on the other side. You will come to another picnic area, the Goat Field, where you will find the striking Taliesin Sculpture, with a noticeboard explaining the story. From here, follow the upper, gravelled path and then the steps, which will take you up on to the road. Turn left to go back into town. *At the end of the churchyard wall, there is a beautifully inscribed piece of slate giving the story of Taliesin in Welsh.* To return to the railway station, pass the fish and chip shop, go up by the Black Lion pub, then follow the outward route back.

Just opposite the church, there is a road (B4389) where you will find a lovely, welcoming café called 'Pippins', which is cosy and family-friendly. It's open *every day except Tuesday* and serves great, home-cooked food. There are also pubs, another café, and a good fish & chip shop.

Ffynnon Fair Well

WALK 2
THE SEVERN VALLEY

DESCRIPTION This is a walk of great contrasts. The first part trails the Offa's Dyke and Severn Way routes, winding through a serene landscape of flat river plain and wide skies. The last part of the walk follows the more intimate towpath of the Montgomery Canal, where the ecology is rich and nature crowds in on all sides. The route follows a level course for most of its length, with only a few short and gentle gradients when using the lanes and also at the locks, where the canal rises/falls with the landscape. This walk is perfectly safe unless the river is in flood (usually in winter), **and should not be attempted at such times**. The landscape around is quickly submerged once the river overflows its banks, and the currents going across the land and the speed of the water flow are extremely dangerous. However, for the greater part of the year, there is no problem. See also **Walk 14**. Allow around 4 hours for this 8¼ mile walk. Also connects with **Walk 5**.
START Powis Arms pub. Grid Ref: SJ 255113
DIRECTIONS From Welshpool go along the A483 Welshpool – Oswestry road (northwards) to Pool Quay and park in the side road, near the Powis Arms pub.

1 Turn left out of the side road and walk up the main road in the Oswestry direction, crossing over at the Dutch barn. Go through the farm gate and over the waymarked stile on the left. Cross the farmland using the easily seen stiles and waymarks, until you reach a small footbridge. Go over and follow the flood embankment, crossing straight over an old railway embankment. *Long since disused, it was once a rail route, built in the mid 19th century, that went between Oswestry and Newtown.*

2 You will now be able to easily follow the flood embankment for the next long stretch of walk, interrupted only by acorn waymarked stiles at field boundaries. *As you walk, the noise of the main road traffic disappears and a sense of remoteness comes in, as the flat and placid river plain dominates. Herons, ducks and swans can be seen all along the Severn here and willows, alder, hawthorn and sycamore lend shade to the riverside. It is a strangely dreamlike landscape. The tall humps of the Breiddons, on the other side of the river, lend contrast but never dominate, and it remains a landscape of vast skies.*

3 After you reach the stile near the metalled lane, the surroundings become more intimate for a while. As the scenery opens out again the embankment (and the route) leaves the river behind. Pass by the metal floodgate and veer left along the small waterway, still following the embankment. At the footbridge continue straight on (you will leave the Offa's Dyke path here), still following the waterway and embankment, passing the double flood control gates on the way. Eventually you will come to a single-track metalled lane. Go straight across and follow the embankment up to the main road.

4 Go straight across, using the stiles, and rejoin the embankment on the other side. Follow the embankment once again, until you reach a metalled lane. Turn right onto the lane and follow it until you come to a canal bridge ahead. Turn left immediately before the bridge and join the canal towpath, turning left along it to Burgedin locks ahead.

5 At the locks there is a recently restored lock keeper's cottage. *Here, as at so many other lock keepers cottages, there is an attached pigsty. It was the usual addition to many rural workers' homes right up until recent times, for those families lucky enough to be able to keep a pig. By the far side of the lock cottage you can see a disused arm of the canal, which once went to Guilsfield, but is now full of water plants and wildlife. There is another set of locks and then a quiet run of towpath between trees of alder, hawthorn, hazel, field maple and oak. The edges of the canal are rich with water-loving plants such as reeds and bulrushes, and wildlife abounds. Ducks, swans and herons are a common sight. The towpath is some-*

WALK 2

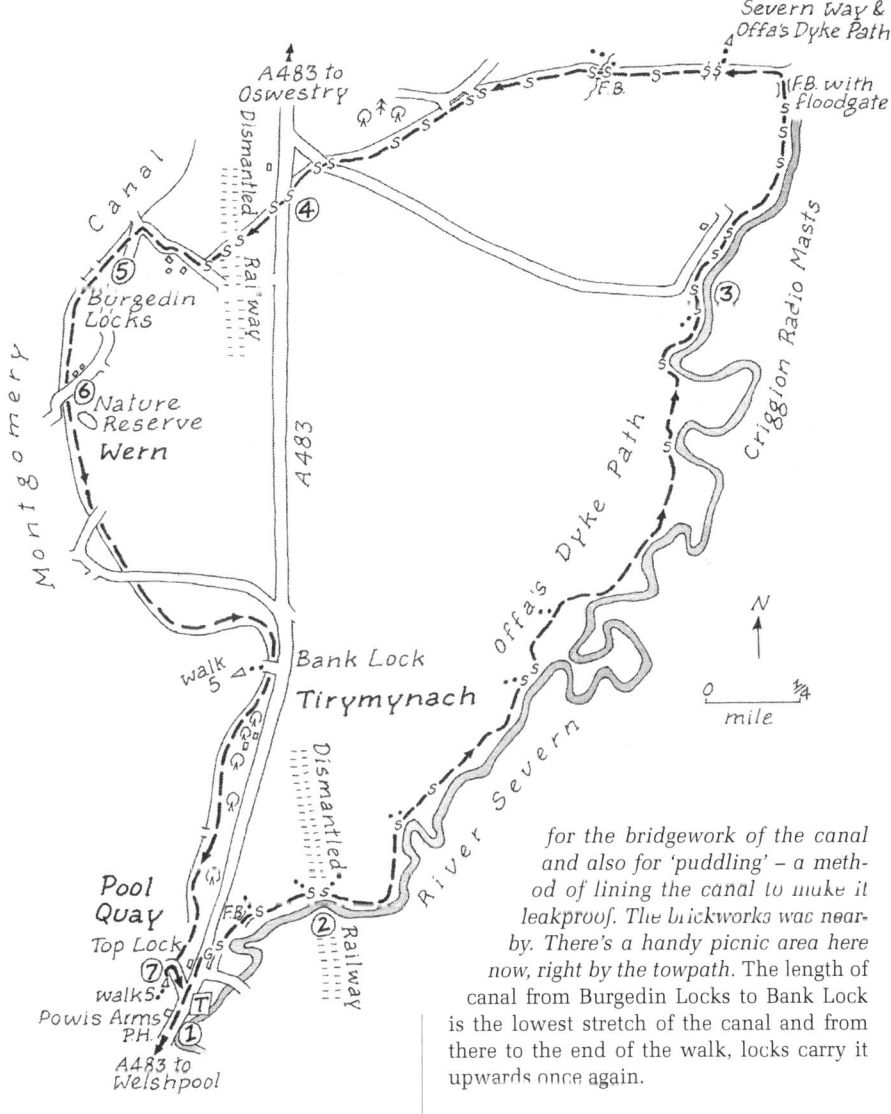

for the bridgework of the canal and also for 'puddling' – a method of lining the canal to make it leakproof. The brickworks was nearby. There's a handy picnic area here now, right by the towpath. The length of canal from Burgedin Locks to Bank Lock is the lowest stretch of the canal and from there to the end of the walk, locks carry it upwards once again.

7 At Top Lock (the only one with a lock keeper's cottage on the towpath side) turn off down the lane to rejoin the main road, where you turn right. *The Powis Arms, and the end of the walk, is just a short way along. Open 11.00 – 23.00 all year, there is a warm welcome for all here, though sadly no meals are served.*

times enclosed in trees and shrubs, and at other times lies open for fine views of the Breiddons on the left, with rolling farmland to the right.

6 The Wern Claypit Nature Reserve lies partway along the route and is worth a diversion. *The clay was used to make bricks*

WALK 3
POWIS CASTLE AND ESTATE

DESCRIPTION This is an easy walk and good at any time of year. For the most part it is a comfortable saunter along fairly level tarmac paths and sturdy towpath, with just a short and gentle rise and fall across well-signposted fields. The scenery around Powis Castle is typical of most estates, having well-tended parkland with many fine mature trees, some native to Britain, and also some specimen trees. You are quite likely to see deer roaming through, as well as swans, ducks and herons on the lake and ponds you will pass. If you have the time, it is possible to visit Powis Castle and Gardens by diverting temporarily from the walk; this fine National Trust property is well worth a visit and can be a day out in itself. There are many well-furnished rooms, fine gardens, a plant shop and excellent tearoom. The canal and canal-side is full of wildlife and always pleasant to walk along. Allow about 2½ hours for this 4¼ mile walk. Also connects with **Walk 14** at Belan lock.

START The gated entry into the Powis Estate land. Grid Ref: SJ 222074

DIRECTIONS Park in Welshpool, either at the Somerfield or Spar car park (both long-stay) and make your way to the crossroads in the centre of town. Go up the main street, pass the Town Hall (on your right) and, a little way after, take the next lane on the left (used for parking). Walk down past the parked cars to the large wrought iron gate at the end.

Powis Castle is *open afternoons from late March to November (closed Tues & Wed)*. It is best to check first before going – ring 01938 551944

1 Go through the gate and follow the path through the grounds. *Down on your left you might catch sight of Llyn Du, a rather beautiful lake, almost hidden by trees in the summer, but at other times of the year reveal-* ing its serene and secret face. Then it looks magnificent, showing stark reflections of the tall trees lining its bank. Walk on until you reach a fork in the path.

2 Turn left (the right hand path will take you to the Castle if you are visiting). This path winds round the front of the Castle and will give you fine views both of the Castle itself, and also eastwards across to Long Mountain. Turn left when you reach the Estate offices and continue until you reach a lane. Go straight across and through the gate opposite (waymarked).

3 Head straight across the field and follow the track, faint at first, downhill until you reach the bridge. Go across and continue straight up (waymarked). At the far end of the field go over the stile and continue straight ahead, following the path between the trees. Go through the gate at the bottom, turn left and cross over the canal bridge. Turn right onto the towpath and right again to follow it back to Welshpool, passing the top one of the two Belan Locks.

4 A short diversion at this lock, by the picnic site, will take you to the disused lime kilns. *Built between 1790 and 1840 they, like all the lime kilns along the canal, converted raw limestone, brought by canal from the Llanymynech Quarries to the north of Welshpool, into slaked lime. This was then distributed throughout the area to improve the agricultural land locally.* To continue, rejoin the towpath and follow it back to Welshpool.

5 At the Safeway car park, you can either head back to town, or follow the canal a short distance to the Canal Centre and Powysland Museum. *Open daily in summer, but only on Saturday afternoons in winter.*

6

WALK 3

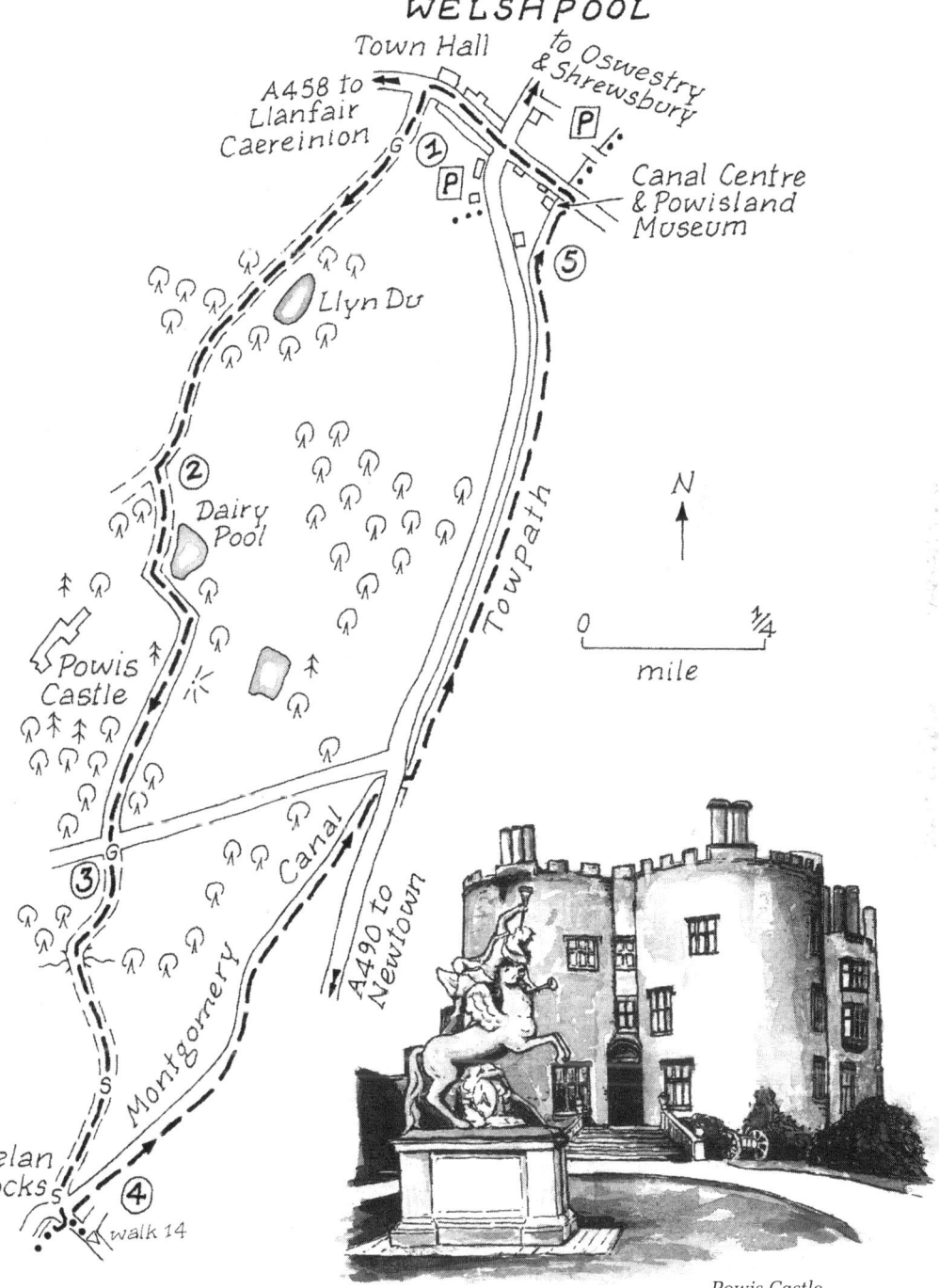

Powis Castle

WALK 4
MOEL Y GOLFA & A ROMANY CHELL

DESCRIPTION A walk for romantics, and connoisseurs of mixed woodland. The three hills of the Breiddons near Welshpool, of which Moel Y Golfa is one, poke up from the flattened plain of the Severn in such a dramatic way that they are an easy landmark for miles around. Each hill has its own character and Moel Y Golfa has the distinction of being mostly covered in lush, mixed woodland, with a double rocky mound near the top; hence it's name, which means bare or bald hill. There are two very short and easy, airy scrambles on this walk (the bare bits), with some steep stretches of path and a few boggy patches, but all are quite easy to negotiate. Any discomforts are more than made up for by the sheer enchantment to be found on much of this route. Also, it's waymarked at virtually every turn. Allow 2 hours for this 3 mile walk. Approximately 1 mile of lane connects this walk with **Walk 8**, should you feel fit and energetic!
START Grid Ref: SJ 283119
DIRECTIONS Travelling from Welshpool, take the A458 to Shrewsbury. From the roundabout where it connects with the A483 to Oswestry, go for 3¾ miles until you reach the bus shelter on the left, at Trewern. Take the first left after the shelter and go half a mile up this winding lane, ignoring the left fork, and you will see a footpath sign on the right. If you are coming by car there is a small area here for parking, but please park sensibly, as the track is in use.

1 Take the grassy path on the left and you will immediately be into a lovely patch of mixed woodland. It's interesting at any time of year, but looks particularly fine in high summer, with great spires of foxgloves soaking the area in dazzling pink spatters. Ignore the path joining from the left and continue upwards into what becomes tall beech woodland.

2 At the next path junction, go over the stile and turn left up the blackberry-lined track. Look out for the next waymark on the left, just as the track seems to be petering out, and continue as directed. The vista opens out as the trees thin and a field appears on the left, allowing views down to the Severn Valley. At the end of the path turn left onto the forestry track and after about 50 yards take the right hand path that leads upwards through the beech trees. The way is not apparent here, but the ground is open and easy (if steep), so head generally for the skyline. Veer left towards the top, where the path is just visible again and follow it along and up the ridge, through a stand of young ash trees.

3 From here to the top, the trees are stunted by the prevailing south-westerlies, and look amazing – like the trees in Japanese paintings. Wonderfully expansive views are opening up now, and it's tempting to stand and stare. There's the whale-like length of Long Mountain close by, with the Arans and the Berwyns far off into Wales and the Long Mynd, in England, pushing up the south-eastern horizon. The first of the quick scrambles over rock comes up now, and is soon dealt with. Then there is a small, flat, grassy patch before the last of the scrambles, and another patch of grass and heather to follow. The last bit of walk to the summit is easy and at this point the grand view is very nearly 360 degrees, only being obscured to the east by treetops.

4 The top of this hill has three humps, the middle one of which has on it an amazing granite monument, surrounded by railings. There are two plaques in memory of two Romany Chells (Gypsy Kings), one being the son of the other. The son, who had the memorial raised in honour of his father, is now himself remembered in the remarkable words carved on the newer plaque. 'Uriah was a fighter for the weak, good to the poor, teacher to the ignorant and a true legend in his own time.' There's more, but I won't spoil it; it's worth the walk just to see this monument. There's a footnote to all this. The story goes that when the final stones of the gypsy

WALK 4

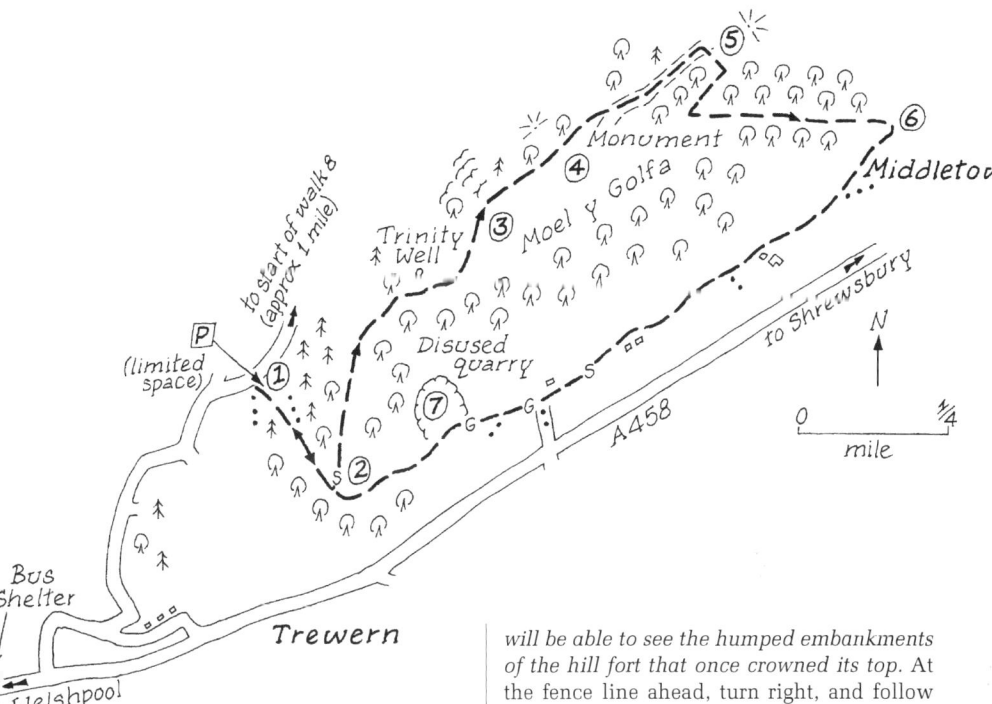

monument were to be taken up and raised into position, several labourers, drinking at a pub in Wellington (a town just beyond Shrewsbury), were 'kidnapped', taken to Moel Y Golfa, and made to do the work before they were let go. A local farmer, who was not kidnapped, was employed to do the finishing work. The ruin of a defunct radio mast lies about, but it doesn't detract from the wonder and interest of this monument. To continue the walk, take the path off the third mound and follow the ridge down through more woodland. It briefly gives way to a stand of bracken, which grows to a voluptuous 6 feet tall by late summer. Just here it is possible to see the Ironbridge Gorge Power Station far off in the south-east, puffing out brilliant white steam into the air, making white fluffy clouds. The path then falls gracefully down into deeper woodland.

5 As the trees clear, a sudden and stunning view of Middleton Hill (part of **Walk 8**) lies straight ahead. If you look carefully, you will be able to see the humped embankments of the hill fort that once crowned its top. At the fence line ahead, turn right, and follow the path down. It zigzags through the steep woodland floor, seemingly forever, but since the wood is fairly open it's not easy to get lost, even when the path is rather faint.

6 At the bottom, the path joins a track. Turn right and follow the flat course between the base of the hill and the fields that front the A458. There are several houses along the way, and at one point the path becomes a mown, grassy track. On passing the last house go through a gate, where the path divides. Take the rising path into the woodland, go through the next gate and you will come to the small, disused quarry.

7 Quiet and deserted, it's a fine, almost theatrical amphitheatre, with a high, ledged rock face that holds gorse, birch and rowan trees. Many birds use the area and their calls are eerily amplified as they fly through. On leaving the quarry the track rises steadily, curving to the right, and is soon heavily lined with blackberry bushes. After a short bend take the left fork and so rejoin the original path, back to the start.

WALK 5
POOL QUAY

DESCRIPTION The first and last stretches of this walk follow the Montgomery Canal towpath. These are the flat bits – the rest of the walk follows Coppice Lane uphill at a moderate rate and then down through well waymarked farmland. Coppice Lane is very quiet, lined with some lovely mixed hedging and has fine views at the top, across patchwork farmland. The towpath, as with the rest of the Montgomery Canal, is lush with waterside flora and fauna and lined with tall native trees, making this a very pleasant walk for a hot day. This 4½ mile walk can easily be accomplished in 2½ hours. Also connects with **Walk 2** and **Walk 6**.
START Powis Arms pub. Grid Ref: SJ 255113
DIRECTIONS From Welshpool, go along the A483 Welshpool-Oswestry road (northwards) to Pool Quay and park near the Powis Arms pub.

*P**ool Quay was*, by the late eighteenth century and through into the nineteenth, a thriving port for the River Severn, which was then navigable up to this point. A massive weir was put across it by the Cistercian monks of nearby Strata Marcella Abbey (built in 1170), and this prevented navigation further upstream. The weir was carried away by a flood in 1881. The abbey is long since gone, having been demolished in the reign of Henry VIII. No trace of it remains except for a few artefacts, including the baptismal font and a doorway arch, which are now in Buttington Church. In the landscape, there are only names to give a clue that it was ever here, such as Abbey Farm, Abbey Barn, and Abbey lift bridge over the canal. But it was the draining of what was then marshland, in order to build the canal, that caused the eventual silting up of the River Severn here and Pool Quay fell into decline. A corn mill, a large (five-storey) woollen mill, a lead-crushing mill and smeltery, sawmills and a barytes mill were all operating around here, but today there is no sign left of any of these.

1 Go left and up the main road in the Oswestry direction, then take the first lane on the left (waymarked). At the top veer left, which will take you to the canal at Top Lock. Turn right onto the towpath and follow it, passing a further two locks, until you reach Bank Lock.

2 At Bank Lock, come off the towpath by the stile, turn left over the canal bridge and go up Coppice Lane. Although the lane is not steep, you will quickly rise high enough to gain some good views of the surrounding countryside. *At the top you will have grand views of the Brieddons, whilst on the other side, there is a panorama of rolling farmland with its hilly backdrop.* Carry on along the road until you reach Dippers Barn on the left.

3 Go over the waymarked stile (just before you reach the garden of the converted barn) and then over the next two stiles. You will now see the next stile diagonally right across the field. Go over this and head across to the small conifer wood. Go over the waymarked stile and down through the wood.

4 Go over the stile at the bottom and look for a further waymarked stile just down the dip ahead. Once over this stile, head diagonally down the field to the stile at the bottom right hand corner. Follow the sunken track through the trees, and then again head diagonally down this field to its lower far corner. The canal borders the bottom of this field and the stile is right next to the canal. Go over this and follow the track along the canal-side, going over another stile until you reach the lift bridge. *It's rather plain in design but so beautiful in its operation. When a boat comes along the canal, the heavy bridge is easily manually raised to allow the boat to pass beneath.*

5 Go over the stile by the gate, cross the bridge, turn left and follow the towpath back to Pool Quay, passing behind the houses as you reach it. Continue until you reach Top Lock, where you meet with the outward route. Take the lane back down to the main road, turn right and you are quickly back at the Powis Arms.

WALK 5

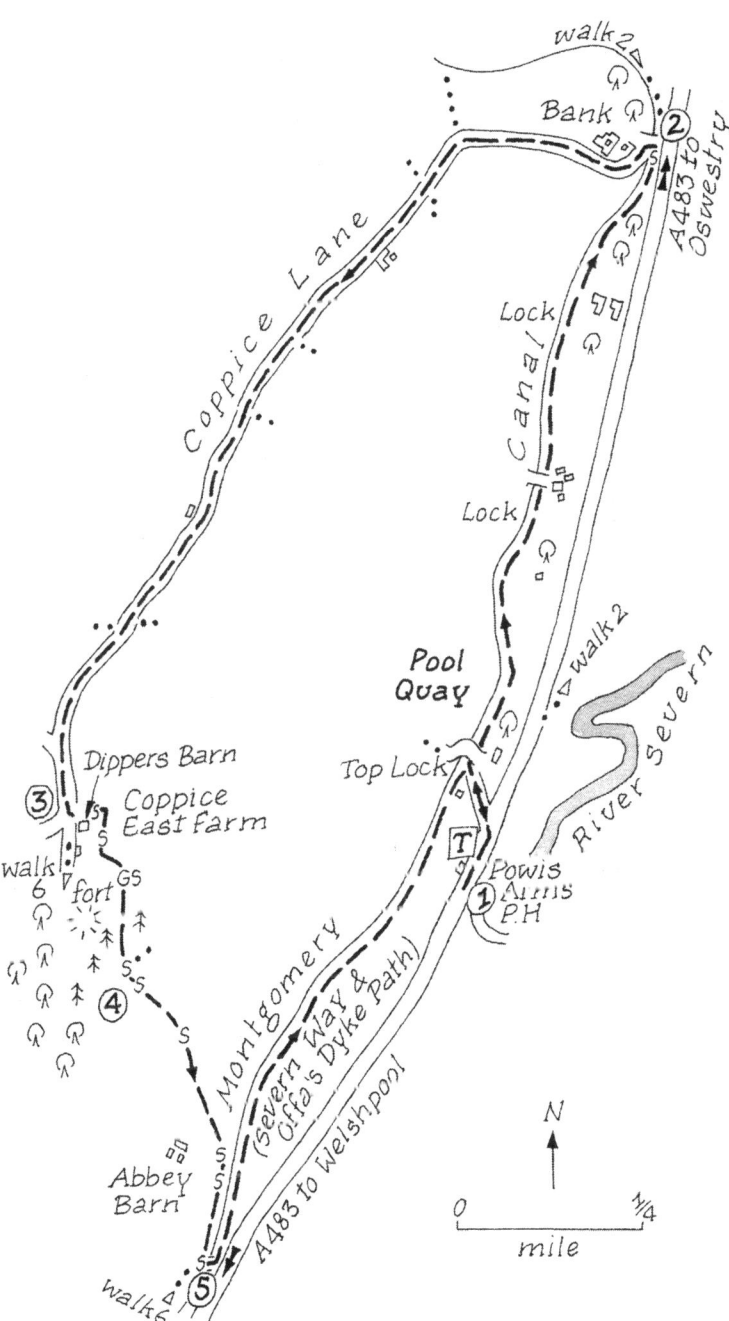

WALK 6
WOODS & QUIET LANES

DESCRIPTION This is a good route if you would like to catch a flavour of what it must have been like to walk the area in the nineteenth century. The first part follows the Montgomery Canal, starting by the old limekilns and leaving it at a swing bridge. It then climbs up through fields to follow tracks which never became metalled lanes, and metalled lanes that, with half-closed eyes, become tracks again, so quiet and leafy are they. It's very easy to pretend to be in the nineteenth century and the whole landscape hints at a bucolic idyll that never really existed, but it's fun to pretend. From the top of the Rhallt, there is a gentle and steady drop down through pleasant farmland on the other side and a quietly pretty lane to finish. Allow 2½ hours to enjoy this 4 mile walk. Also connects with **Walk 5**.

START Parking space at the limekilns, by the canal. Grid Ref: SJ 241088

DIRECTIONS Head out of Welshpool on the A458. Turn left at the roundabout, up the narrow lane and immediately right (before the canal bridge). Park in the area by the limekilns. Alternatively, you can walk from Welshpool either by road or, and probably nicer, you can walk along the canal from the back of the Spar car park.

Take a few moments, if you can, to look at the limekilns, before you start the walk. It's difficult to believe that this quiet area was once a hive of activity. Raw limestone used to be brought along the canal by narrowboat from Llanymynech Quarries, for burning in the kilns to make agricultural lime. A number of other businesses also traded here, including the selling of coal. The canal itself, after many years of neglect, was saved and is being beautifully restored, due to the great efforts of British Waterways and a number of voluntary organisations. These days all is peaceful and there is a picnic area where there was once a wharf.

1 To start the walk, go onto the towpath and turn right to follow it. *The first part is well tree-lined on both sides, cool and shady in summer with the branches meeting over the water, and delightful in all seasons. After the first lift bridge the woods on the left, towering over the canal, will be the ones you look down on at the highest section of the walk. After passing the footbridge, the canal widens and there is a lovely stretch of wetland on the opposite bank. Crack willows abound, with reeds, ferns and a tangle of deciduous trees at the margins making a wonderful habitat for all sorts of wildlife. It is at this point that the trees on the right drop away, giving lovely views of Long Mountain opposite.* (**Walk 15** *takes you to Beacon Hill, on its summit.*)

2 Cross over the canal by the swing bridge ahead, go over the stile on the left and turn right, following the canal on the opposite side now, until you reach the next stile. Go over this one, and also the next stile directly ahead. Then head diagonally up towards a clump of trees pushing out into the field. Go through the trees, over the stile and then walk more or less straight up this field to the stile lying just under the short steep bank. Go up the bank, over the next stile ahead and through the conifer wood. Go over the stile at the end, then head diagonally up towards the next stile. Make your way round the converted barn (Dippers Barn), using the stiles and waymarks until you reach the metalled lane. (The last section from the canal to this point is shared with Walk 5). Turn left.

3 At this point the lane becomes an unmade track. Follow it up into the beautiful mixed woodland ahead. *The trees are mainly beeches and oaks, with hawthorn and elder at the edges. At the junction, carry straight on up; it's marked as a bridle path. It's here that the twenty-first century fades away and the nineteenth century idyll shimmers in the mind as the path winds on ahead.*

4 At the next junction, there is a strangely shaped old oak tree, *which could easily be included in a fairy story landscape.* Turn

WALK 6

left here and follow the track until you reach a wide gate. Go through the side gate and then almost immediately go over the next stile on the left, leaving the track. Walk up the field and past the waymark. *Down on your right are lovely views of the surrounding countryside, including Gaer Fawr hill* **(Walk 7)** *with the village of Guilsfield spread out along the near valley bottom.* Cross the stile at the end of this field and follow the hedge line along the base of the hill, although many people divert up to the summit.

5 *From here, there are terrific 360° views. There is the broad flank of Long Mountain to the east, the abrupt bulk of the Breiddons rising off the floor of the Severn Valley to the north with the Cheshire Plain beyond and, in the west, the dramatic sweep of the mountain horizon heading into Mid-Wales.* From the Trig Point, go straight down the hillside, on your left, and rejoin the path. Follow it up and over the hill with the mobile phone aerial on it, keeping to the fence line (and behind the aerial). At the top corner of the field, go over the waymarked stile. Roughly follow the fence line again to the bottom and then up the next field (these fields are ungated). At the waymark post in the middle of the next field, go diagonally downhill to the right corner. Go over the stile and along the fence line by the conifer wood to the bottom. Go over the next stile and through a small and beautiful strip of mixed woodland.

6 At the bottom go over the stile, cross the lane and over another stile, heading straight across the field to the next stile. Go across the next field to its bottom right corner, go over the stile and turn left down the lane. *As the sides of the lane become steeper, so the trees meet overhead to make a quietly romantic ending to this walk.*
At the bottom, go over the bridge to the limekilns and picnic area.

13

WALK 7
GAER FAWR HILL
Woodland and a hill fort

DESCRIPTION Not far in miles walked, but nevertheless well worth a visit and a really good choice if you are accompanied by children, with some of the best and most beautiful ancient mixed woodland to be seen. The way is moderately steep at times, but the paths are good and anyone who is averagely fit, children included, can easily achieve the walk to the top. Once there, it is possible to get lovely views of the surrounding hills and countryside. Picnics recommended here, or you can get meals either in Guilsfield or at the Derwen Garden Centre, which you pass on the B4392. At an approximate 1½ miles, allow around 2 hours for this walk through truly enchanting woodland.

START Car park at Gaer Fawr Hill. Grid Ref: SJ 219125

DIRECTIONS Leave Welshpool on the A458 westwards, going up the main street. At the roundabout at the top of Welshpool turn right onto the A490, signposted for Guilsfield. After one and a half miles turn right onto the B4392 to Guilsfield; you pass the Derwen Garden Centre along here. At the junction in Guilsfield, turn right and follow this road for about half a mile. Just as you leave the houses behind, turn left and up the lane signposted for Geuffordd. (The signpost is on the right hand side, although the turning is on the left.) Stop after about a third of a mile, at the disused quarry on the right, now a car parking area for Gaer Fawr Hill and woods.

Two thousand years ago, Gaer Fawr Hill had a Celtic encampment on its summit. Around AD 50, the Roman Twentieth Legion arrived, defeated the Celtic tribes in the area and the encampment ceased to be occupied. In 1984, the Woodland Trust bought the site and now it is an important archaeological, woodland and wildlife conservation area. The summit of the hill is still surrounded by the earthen embankments of the hill fort.

There are seats at various intervals, some carved with the footprints of wild animals, and a very unusual one at the top; it's shaped as an oblong stool, with a boar's head at either end. The inspiration for this has come from a small bronze boar found in the vicinity, thought to be either Celtic or Roman.

1 Take the gated entrance to the left and enter the woodland. The paths are easy on the feet and waymarked. Generally, make your way upwards. Should you take a wrong turning, you will still meet up with the route again and there are several paths to the top. The early part of the walk is the steepest, the way down on the eastern side is gradual, though longer. *Almost all the trees here have been coppiced down to the ground in the past and now they sport many-trunked shapes. There are oak, birch, ash, rowan, hawthorn, holly and willow, amongst others. The coppiced hazel has sprouted up into great thick brushes, making wonderful habitats for wildlife.*

2 At the top, look for the double-headed boar seat, sitting incongruously in the woods. From there, make your way southwards along the ridge and down through a slightly different woodland. *There are crowds of tall, pencil-straight trees here, all wound round with ivy, making them look like a collection of woodland maypoles. Also, look out for a seat carved in the shape of an oak leaf.* You will eventually come out at the other gate in the car parking area. This walk can, of course, be done the other way round if you prefer.

The Oak in Guilsfield has a large outside seating area and a children's play area. It is open every day from 12.00 – 23.00, and meals are served from 12.00 – 24.00 and 18.30 – 21.00.
The King's Head has a small garden and is open from 12.00 – 15.00 and 17.30 – 23.00, all day on Fri, Sat and Sun. They also serve meals.
The Derwen Garden Centre is open every day from 10.00 – 18.00, except Tuesday, when it open from 14.00 – 18.00. There is a

good restaurant and a conifer maze that's fun for children and adults alike.

Guilsfield also has some lovely old buildings, including a fine church and churchyard.

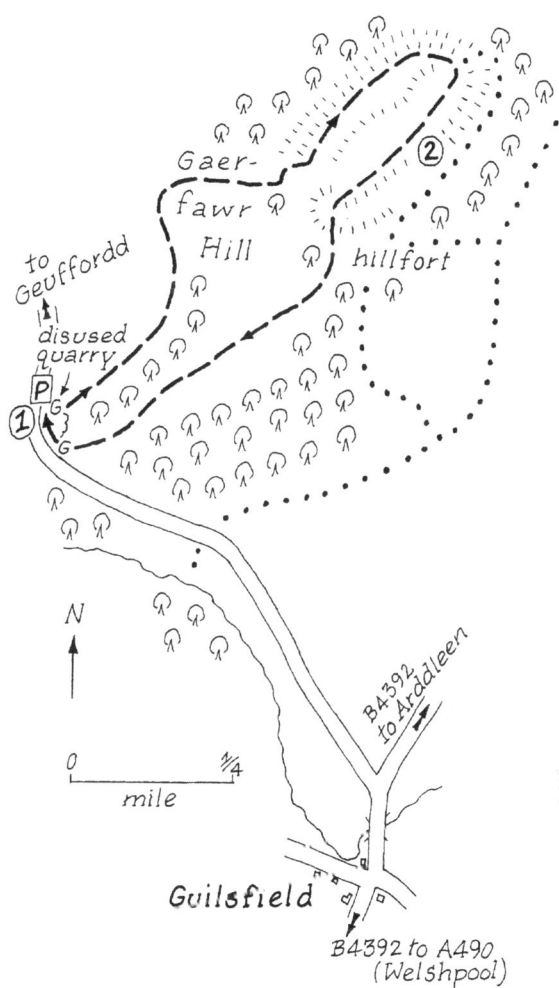

About the author, Kirsten Spencer

After a lifetime of living in numerous English towns and cities, sometimes on houseboats, she 'discovered' Wales, and moved across the border twelve years ago. She then lived on Long Mountain, near Welshpool, and from here she enthusiastically explored Wales and its culture.

She writes both fiction and non-fiction, and her other passions include beekeeping, landscape history, photography and botany. She now lives in Ceredigion.

WALK 8
MIDDLETOWN HILL & BREIDDON HILL

DESCRIPTION The two hills on this walk are next to Moel Y Golfa (**Walk 4**) and make up the remaining main heights of the Breiddon Hills. This is a walk with many twists and turns to it, having almost constant views, with terrific panoramas from both hill summits and ever-changing surroundings with, inevitably, some steep stretches of path to negotiate. If you are a moderately fit person though, don't be put off, as the walk is worth the effort. Combining the two hills will give you a chance to really stretch your legs, though small children might find it too much. Allow 4½ hours for this more strenuous 4¾ mile walk. For the madly fit and energetic, approximately 1 mile of lane connects this walk with **Walk 4**.

START Car parking area at Middletown Hill. Grid Ref: SJ 297130

DIRECTIONS From Welshpool, take the A458 towards Shrewsbury, turning right at the roundabout where it connects with the A483 to Oswestry. Continue on the A458 for 3¾ miles until you reach the bus shelter on the left, at Trewern. Take the first left after the shelter and go up the lane for 1½ miles, where there is a good car parking area on the right, at the base of Middletown Hill.

*M*iddletown Hill is an open, grassy dome, whose summit holds the remains of a hill fort embankment. It makes for a very good day out in its own right, being a wonderful spot for kite flying and an airy picnic, so is great for families. It's equally good for a quiet ramble, having its own peculiar ambience – an 'airy serenity'. In complete contrast, Breiddon Hill slumbers beneath conifer and mixed woodlands, with a small lake, the remains of a prehistoric field settlement and several open stretches on the walk. The breezy top is crowned with Rodney's Pillar, erected by local landowners as a 'thank-you' to Admiral Rodney for his use of Montgomeryshire oak for the ships of the Royal Navy.

1 Walk directly up Middletown Hill from the parking area, using the very wide grassy track between the stands of bracken. The route up is obviously steep, but there are a number of flat bits and a saddle on the way up, where you can catch your breath and admire the expanding views. At the top, the path goes through what remains of the ramparts and distinctive gateways that lead in and out of the hill fort area. At the other side of the hill fort, follow the path on down. When you reach the fence line, turn left and continue on, winding down through an open stand of young trees, mostly oak, rowan, ash, hawthorn, blackthorn and coppiced hazel.

2 At the bottom, turn left along the lane for about 500 yards, until you reach the next farm. Go down the driveway and turn right, keeping the barns to your left. Climb over the low fence ahead (breeze blocks have been placed here to help the short-legged), and follow the fence line to the woods ahead.

3 Cross the excellent footbridge over the ditch, go over the stile and along the path. Turn right when you reach the track and follow it, skirting the edge of some beech woodland (it can be a bit muddy here). At the top of this track, turn right onto the main track and follow it round past stands of conifer and mixed woodland. Just ahead is a junction. Take the right turn and look out for a waymarked bridle path on the left. Take this path, which goes up between beeches on one side and a conifer stand on the other.

4 Where the path divides, take the left path and continue upwards. Rodney's Pillar can now be seen directly up ahead. This path threads up and across open land between stands of conifer. Go over the stile ahead, continue up, then go over the next stile and head up through the thin stand of trees to the summit and Rodney's Pillar – the route is well waymarked.

WALK 8

6 Go through the metal gate ahead and follow this wide and grassy path. *Above and behind are the scant remains of a prehistoric settlement and field system.* Go through the next gate, along to the crossroads ahead and go straight across onto the next grassy path (waymarked).

7 Look for a small lake through the trees on the left. *It is prettily fringed all round with reeds and has a rather lovely, tiny island in the middle, sprouting a tiara of silver birch trees.* Carry on along the path into the conifer woods. At the end of this path, turn right as waymarked. The route is now on a wide break through some striking mature conifer woodland. Past thinning of the lowest branches has allowed for dim vistas through the trees, and there is a real fairytale quality to this part of the walk. Look for the diverging paths and take the one on the left, which rises and wanders charmingly through mixed conifers. At one point there are wonderful, almost alpine views across the steep valley below to Breiddon Hill, now opposite.

8 Go straight across the clearing (imagine it as a traffic roundabout and take the third exit), into more conifer woodland. The path is lined on the left with old and wonderfully gnarled and mossy deciduous trees, marking an old stone field wall (still just visible in places). These amazing trees are the remains of an ancient hedge. The track now takes you gradually down along the ridge and then veers left and down to the bottom.

9 Go through the gate, round the renovated house and along the track to the lane. Turn left and go along the lane until you are back at the car parking area below Middletown Hill.

5 Look for the footpath that takes you along the ridge. *A short way along it there is a really good stone compass, put there by the Rotary Club, which shows the directions for all the hills and mountains to be seen, with their distance away in miles. On a clear day you can see as far as Cadair Idris, which is almost at the coast, to Snowdon in the north-west, and Ironbridge Power Station many miles away to the east, in the English hills.* To continue the walk, carry on along the path to the waymark post. *You may hear the dull rumblings of machinery and stone being moved, rising up from the depths of Criggion Quarry, over to your right. At 580 feet, it was once the highest single quarry face in Britain, though recent developments have interrupted this sheer face with a system of stepping.* The path now drops steadily down through mixed light woodland to a waymarked crossroads.

17

WALK 9
GALLT YR ANCR
Anchorite's Hill

DESCRIPTION A short but challenging walk, the route climbs sharply up from the north-east, via a winding set of steps, and then follows a narrow ridge. There are some steep wooded drops to either side, but, as long as you keep to the path, there is no problem. The woods on the way up are of mixed deciduous and evergreen trees, notably oaks, beeches and yews, with an undergrowth of bilberry and heather; the path winds enchantingly through it all. In contrast, the summit of Gallt yr Ancr is grassy and bare, save for a number of small but deep holes, allegedly wells that have never run dry. It is remarkably quiet and expansive up here and so very well worth the effort, with a stunning panorama stretching in all directions. One can only guess at the remarkable views to be seen unknown thousands of years ago, when the atmosphere was crystal clear and the first inhabitants of the area stood on these heights. Allow 2 hours or so for this 2 mile, initially strenuous, walk. Also connects with **Walk 10**.

START The car park at Meifod (toilets). Grid ref: SJ 153132

DIRECTIONS From Welshpool, take the A490 northwards, signposted for Llanfyllin. After a little over 3 miles, turn left onto the Meifod road (signposted) and follow it to Meifod. This route makes for a really nice drive through lovely scenery, and passes an almost hidden lake, Llyn Du. Tan-y-Llyn Nurseries is also on the route; they are part of the National Gardens Scheme, with three acres of garden and orchard. At the junction, turn right, then take the next left and park in the free car park (signposted).

1 Turn right out of the car park and walk on past the village hall for a short distance, until you reach the road called Pentre Barog. On the left, opposite this road, take the path on the left immediately after the house called 'Malwen', and before the old black-and-white timbered house. The path (not waymarked) looks a bit like someone's driveway – but isn't. Where the path divides, turn right, go up a few steps, over the stile and follow the steep steps round and up onto the ridge. Follow the path along the ridge and when it dips a little, look for the waymarked signpost. Veer left and follow the path, going over a stile. It is normal here to divert slightly to the summit.

2 Up here is the promised panorama. To the east, the River Vyrnwy snakes along the valley below, and the Breiddons (Walks 4 and 8) are just visible over the tops of the near hills. The wide spread of the Cheshire Plain lies away to the north, whilst the long rim of hills on the southern horizon leads the eye round to the mountains of West Wales. Cadair Idris, which is near the coast, and the sheer flanks of the Arans are easily visible on a moderately clear day. From here, carry on along the top to the lesser summit, and then down into the saddle between this and the lower hill ahead. Turn left here (don't go up the lower hill), and follow the widening path down and around the base of the lower hill.

3 Down at the fence ahead there is a tall post (waymarked) sticking up from the fence at the corner. Turn right (you are now on Glyndŵr's Way) and follow the path along, going through a gate and on down through woodland until you reach the gate at the lane. Walk along the lane (also part of Glyndŵr's Way), and then turn right at the road junction and back to the car park.

Meifod village is well worth exploring. There is an inn, The King's Head, serving lunches, dinners and real ale. Opposite is the church of St Tysilio and St Mary, which has a carved Celtic coffin lid along by the south aisle.

There is now a Kittiwake guide detailing 20 fine walks around the village.

WALK 9

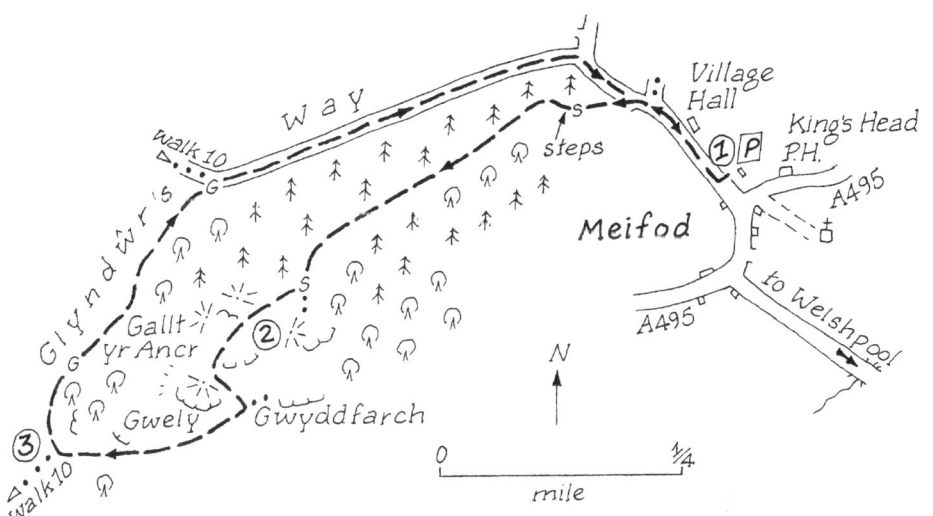

Meifod

WALK 10
MEIFOD TO PONTROBERT

DESCRIPTION This would be a good walk for any time of year, though it is inclined to be a bit muddy in places in winter. It is excellent for a summer's day outing. Starting from Meifod, the outward route takes you below Gallt yr Ancr (**Walk 9**) and follows Glyndŵr's Way across gently rolling farmland to the village of Pontrobert, on the banks of the River Vyrnwy. There are no shops here, but The Royal Oak Inn serves food all day from *twelve noon, (you would need to ring first for weekday lunchtimes between New Year and Easter, so they know you are coming)*. The return route takes you onto slightly higher, more wooded ground and along some very quiet, pastoral lanes back to Meifod. Allow around 3 hours or so (more if stopping off at Pontrobert) for this 6¾ mile walk. Also connects with **Walk 9**.

START The car park at Meifod. Grid Ref: SJ 153132

DIRECTIONS From Welshpool, take the A490 northwards. After 3 miles, turn left onto the Meifod road (signposted) and follow it to Meifod. At the junction turn right, then take the next left and park in the free car park (signposted, toilets).

1 Turn right out of the car park, passing the Village Hall, and take the first lane on the left. This will take you behind Gallt yr Ancr Hill. Where the road bends to the right there is a waymarked track on the left. Go through the gate and follow the track up through the trees. Go through another gate and across a long field, using the waymarks and keeping the fence line to your right, until you reach a stile at the lane. Go over, turn right and follow this lane until it bends to the right. Just after this, the road forks.

2 Take the left fork (marked 'No Through Road') and follow this smaller lane down and up again until it turns into a track. Just here there is a waymarked left turn. Take this farm track and turn right over the waymarked stile immediately before reaching the farm buildings.

3 Go left for approximately 50 yards to the waymark post. Follow the track to the end of the field and the next waymark at the fence. Go through and cut across the right-hand corner of the field to the near waymarked gate. Go through and veer left to the bottom of the field, cross the footbridge and go up into the next field to the stile ahead. This stile is unmissable as it stands completely isolated, the old fence around it having been removed. Go over it if you like!

4 Turn left and follow the tree-lined track until you reach the copse of trees ahead. Veer right here, keeping the copse on your left and go up. Walk between the two gateposts ahead (no gate) and go straight up the next field to the stile. Go over and along the top of the next field, keeping the long, narrow copse of evergreen trees to your left. At the waymarked post veer slightly to the right and make for the waymarked gate ahead. There is a concrete animal drinking trough beside it. Go through the gate, across the track and through the gate opposite. Walk straight across and up the field on its highest point.

5 Go to the right hand of the two gates ahead (waymarked). Go over the stile by the gate and follow the track round and down until you come to a lane and crossroads. If you don't want to go down into Pontrobert, you will take a right turn here. Otherwise, turn left and follow the lane down for a short distance, to the Royal Oak Inn. *The village was named after Robert ab Oliver, who built or repaired the bridge after it had been swept away by a great storm in October of 1632 (Pont is Welsh for bridge).*

20

WALK 10

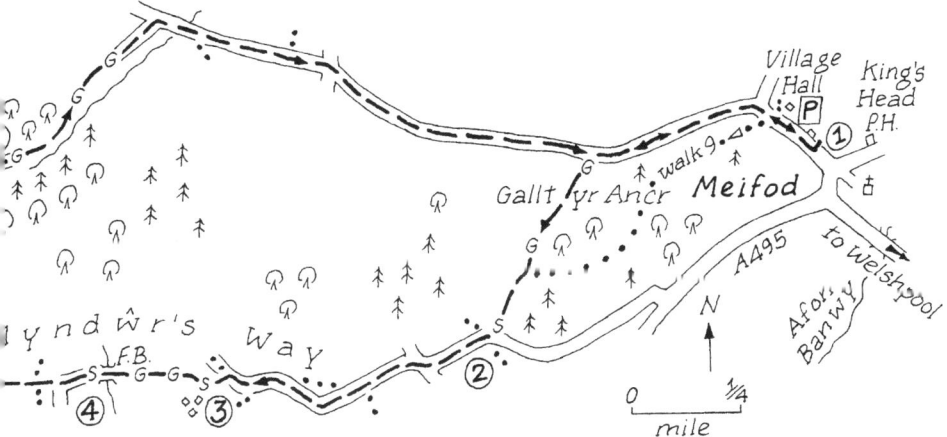

There is a small but interesting report of happenings at Pontrobert, which can be read in the Montgomeryshire Collections, 1896. In 1881, the dissatisfaction in the village at having to pay tithe rents was brought to a head when a cow was seized from the local shoemaker, to pay the tithes. At the auction of the cow, a youngster threw an egg 'of considerable size and antiquity' at the auctioneer, which found its target and 'its delightful fragrance lingered round the spot'. Pontrobert today seems to be less troubled, and is certainly a quiet village with the River Vyrnwy adding charm to this lovely spot.

6 To continue the walk, leave the inn and go back up the lane to the crossroads. Go across and follow this lane, passing some impressively tall conifers looming up from the valley and stream below you, on the left. As the lane leaves the trees and stream behind, look out for a very small, triangular copse of woodland on the right.

7 Pass this and, approximately 30 yards further on, turn right along a farm track. As the laid track ends, take the grassy track on the left and go through the gate behind the small building. Follow round, through the next gate and, where the track reaches a further wooden gate, go through. Follow the path round the base of the hill, keeping the fence line to your right. Go through the gate ahead and walk on to where the path diverges. Go through the gate here and continue in a straight line, keeping the fence line on your left now.

8 Go through the wooden gate at the end of the field and continue following the path around the base of the wooded hill, heading gently upwards, with the stream and other woodland down on your right. Go through the next gate and follow this track along and up to the lane.

9 Turn right and follow the lane, going straight across at the crossroads, and then down and around the base of Gallt yr Ancr, until you reach Meifod again.

See **Walk 9** for more information on Meifod village. The fit and energetic can easily combine **Walks 9** and **10** for a grand day out.

WALK 11
ESTATE LAND, COMMON LAND & HARRIET'S HILL

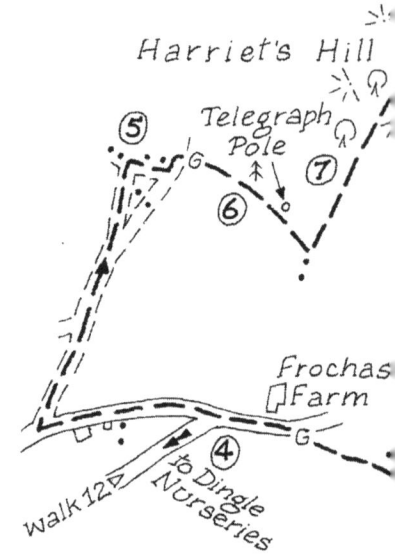

DESCRIPTION This is a comfortable amble through part of the Llanerchydol Estate, across a stretch of common land, up and over Harriet's Hill for some great views, and then back along pleasant and quiet lanes to Welshpool. There is also the chance to visit the Dingle Nurseries if you wish. This walk has the added advantage of needing only your own legs to get to it, as the walk starts and finishes at the top end of Welshpool. Allow 2½ hours for this 4 mile walk. Also connects with **Walk 12** for the first section.

START At the start of the A490 to Guilsfield, just off the roundabout at the junction of the A458 and A490. Grid Ref: SJ 217075

DIRECTIONS Go up the main street through Welshpool (the A458) to the roundabout. The Raven Inn and the Welshpool & Llanfair Light Railway Station are both situated at this roundabout. Take the second exit, the A490, signposted for Guilsfield, and then the lane on the left, signposted for Llanerchydol Estate.

1 From the A490 take the waymarked tarmac lane to the left and go through the gates, following the track around and up until you reach a waymarked right turn to a farm. The way ahead takes you to Y Golfa (**Walk 12**), so turn right instead and follow this farm track, go through a gate, and then veer left around the barn. Cross the stream via the footbridge and then go over the waymarked stile ahead.

2 Follow the hedge line up and round, keeping it to your right. Look out for where this field and two others meet at the stream now below you – you will see a waymarked stile down at the edge of the stream. Go over it and up onto the next field.

3 Go diagonally up the field, aiming for the top left corner. At the top, go through the farm gate and along a very short stretch of track to the lane ahead. Turn left and follow the lane, taking the next right fork ahead. If you want to visit the Dingle Nurseries (*open 09.00-17.00 daily*), take the left fork. There are no toilets or refreshments, though they do sell ice creams *between Easter and autumn*.

4 To continue, take the right fork and go up this lane until you reach a house on the left (a cattery and kennels) and a narrow strip of woodland on the right. Approximately 30 yards further on there is an easily seen, but unmarked, path going up through these trees. Take this path onto the common land and go up the hill. The way soon opens out onto grass and bracken and at the top there are some fine views of the surrounding countryside. Once you are on the top, turn right along the wide path and follow it, going along and then veering left downhill.

WALK 11

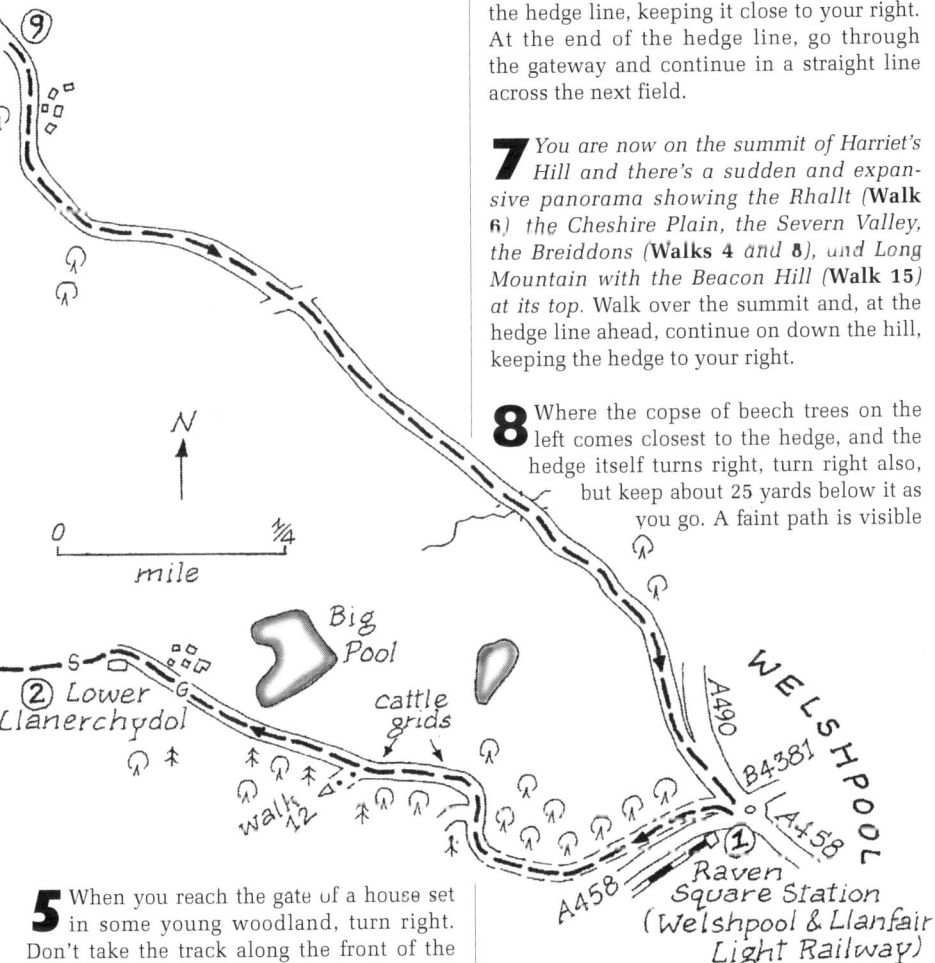

corner. At the bottom, turn left and follow the hedge line, keeping it close to your right. At the end of the hedge line, go through the gateway and continue in a straight line across the next field.

7 You are now on the summit of Harriet's Hill and there's a sudden and expansive panorama showing the Rhallt (**Walk 6**) the Cheshire Plain, the Severn Valley, the Breiddons (**Walks 4 and 8**), and Long Mountain with the Beacon Hill (**Walk 15**) at its top. Walk over the summit and, at the hedge line ahead, continue on down the hill, keeping the hedge to your right.

8 Where the copse of beech trees on the left comes closest to the hedge, and the hedge itself turns right, turn right also, but keep about 25 yards below it as you go. A faint path is visible

5 When you reach the gate of a house set in some young woodland, turn right. Don't take the track along the front of the house that leads downwards: take the track which leads upwards. Ignore the track coming in from the right, further up. When you see the fence line ahead, go right and through the gate. Turn left and follow the field boundary upwards, keeping the trees to your left.

6 When the boundary turns sharp left, leave it and head on up across the field, passing to the right of the telegraph pole in the middle of the field. As the field drops down again, head down to the lower right

in the turf. As the field drops down, head for the trees ahead – you may also be able to see a small reservoir on your right. Go down through the wide grassy bit between the two stands of trees and then through the gate onto the lane.

9 Turn right and follow this lane up to the crossroads. Go straight across and follow this lane (which becomes a track) back towards Welshpool and the starting point.

WALK 12
Y GOLFA

DESCRIPTION A walk with great views and no steep uphill bits! Here is another chance to take a route directly out of Welshpool without using your car, bike or public transport to get to the start. Ponds, parkland and estate tracks predominate the lower parts of the walk. It also follows part of Glyndŵr's Way. From the top of Y Golfa, after a steady and gradual walk uphill, there is arguably the finest panorama to be seen in the area. Allow 3½ hours for this 6½ mile walk. Also connects with **Walk 11**.

START At the start of the A490 to Guilsfield, just off the roundabout at the junction of the A458 and A490. Grid Ref: SJ 217075

DIRECTIONS Go up the main street through Welshpool (the A458) to the roundabout. The Raven Inn and the Welshpool Light Railway are both situated at this roundabout. Take the second exit, the A490, signposted for Guilsfield, and then the lane immediately on the left, signposted for Llanerchydol Estate.

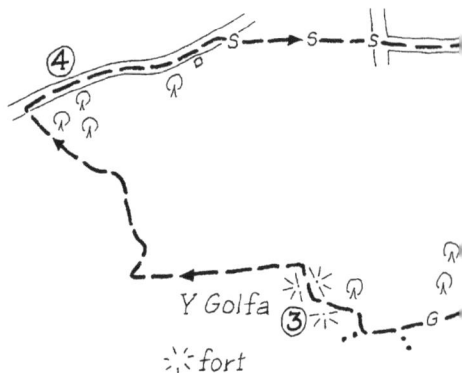

1 Take the left-hand waymarked tarmac lane and go through the gates, following the track round and up until you reach a right turn signposted to Llanerchydol Farm, just after the third cattle grid. This is the point at which you turn off for **Walk 11**. This time, continue straight on and you will be into some pleasant estate parkland. Follow the track through, passing a pond on your left. Don't take the left turn after this, but carry straight on. Follow this main track as it veers left and keep the stone wall to your right.

2 Cross over the cattle grid along this pleasant way and, as you go, look out for a ruined icehouse on your right, on the other side of a stile. Carry on along the main track, going through a farm gate and passing several ponds. Just before you reach the end of the track, where it disappears into the yard of a house, turn right and head approximately 50 yards across the field to a waymarked farm gate. Go through and straight on, keeping closely to the field boundary on your right. Go over the waymarked stile ahead, again keeping the field boundary to your right. At the gate ahead, go through onto common land and follow the grass track on up for about 275 yards, where a waymark will give you directions to the summit.

3 At the top, take some time to enjoy an excellent view of the Breiddons rising up from the Severn valley to the east and some of the distant mountains to the west, including Cadair Idris, the Arans and the Berwyns. Waymarks from the summit direct you downhill, skirting the golf course and passing through the edge of a wood, until you reach the lane at the bottom.

4 Turn right and follow this pretty sunken lane until you reach a barn on the right. Approximately 80 yards further on, and also on the right, there is a gate and stile set back from the lane. Go over the stile and walk ahead, aiming for the few trees (the remains of an old hedge line) in the middle of the field. These will lead you to another stile. Go over and once again follow the trees across the field to the next stile. Go over and continue ahead, now on the tarmac lane. Follow it for a quiet and pleasant amble up and past the Dingle Nurseries (on your right). If

WALK 12

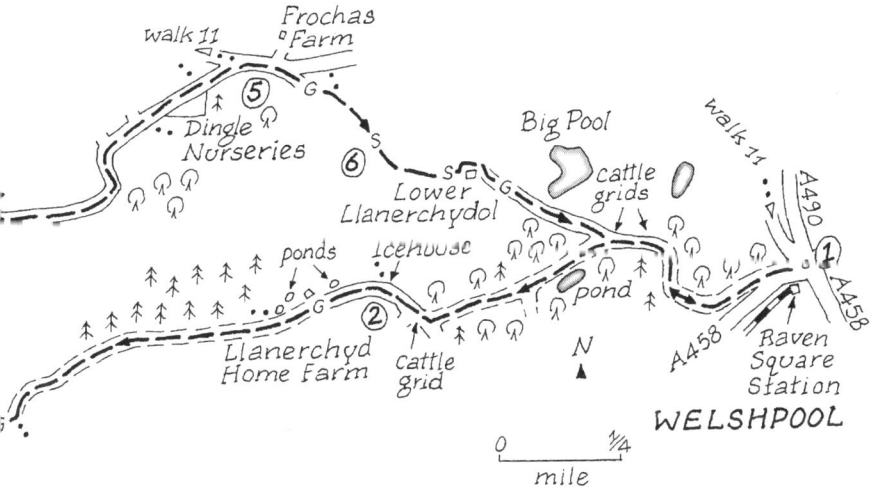

you have the time and energy, it's worth a visit, especially to their gardens (charged for entrance, the proceeds going to charity), though there is no café and no toilets. They do, however, sell icecreams between Easter and autumn.

5 At the junction with the road ahead, you merge with the outward journey from **Walk 11**. Go right and follow this road until you reach Frochas Farm on the left, approximately 100 yards further on. Opposite is a short, grassy track leading obliquely to a farm gate. Take this track, go through the gate and cross the field diagonally down to your left. Leave the field to the right of the bottom left corner.

6 Drop down to the stream, go over the waymarked stile and head into the next field, keeping the hedge line closely to your left. At the end of the field, cross the waymarked stile and follow the track across the stream, round the barn and on until you reach the junction once more. Turn left and retrace your steps back to the start.

WALK 13
BERRIEW

DESCRIPTION This is a walk which not only takes you round some delightful countryside, but also gives you the chance to explore a very pretty village with a long history. It has a broad river (the Rhiw) running through, lending it a dreamy air, plus traditional black-and-white houses, a fine church, a few shops and a number of inns and pubs for lunchtime or evening refreshment. To top it all, there is the wonderfully quirky Andrew Logan Museum of Sculpture. The walk itself goes through pleasant farmland and along an interesting stretch of the Montgomery canal. Allow around 2 hours for this 3¼ mile walk.

START The car park and picnic area by the aquaduct. Grid Ref: SJ 188005

DIRECTIONS Take the A483 south out of Welshpool, heading for Newtown. After approximately four miles turn right down the B4390, signposted for Berriew. Once in the village take the left turn, signposted Museum of Sculpture. Go over the bridge across the river and take the next left. Go past the Museum, under the aquaduct and park in the car park and picnic area immediately after it, on the right.

Famed as the founder of the Alternative Miss World (started in 1972), Andrew Logan has had his work shown in the National Portrait Gallery, international exhibitions and now his own museum. Please visit it if you can, it's well worth the modest entrance fee. Opening times vary according to the time of year, so phone 01686 640689 for an update.

1 Turn left out of the car park, walk up the lane by the river, passing the Andrew Logan Museum, and turn right at the end. Cross over the bridge and turn left at the Post Office (signposted for New Mills). Walk up the lane and take a right turn at the lane signposted Glan Yr Afon, also signed as a No Through Road. Go up the lane and when it veers left, go straight ahead over the waymarked stile and into the field.

2 Walk up the field, keeping the hedge line to your right and the brook to your left. As the field opens out, aim upwards and to the right of the brow of the hill ahead. As you circle round, you will see a fence ahead. Where this fence line joins at the corner of the next field, which juts out into the field you are walking, look for the waymarked stile. Go over, and then over the next stile, which is immediately on your right. Turn left and follow the fence line along and down to the farm gate at the bottom of the field.

3 Go over the stile next to the gate, turn right and follow the track up until you reach a farm gate on the left, with a waymarked stile. Go over and straight across this field into the next, via a gateway. Go straight ahead again to the point where the next field corners out into this one. Climb easily over the short length of barred wooden fence. It's not waymarked on this side, though it is on the other (a stile has been requested). Continue on, keeping the hedge line to your left, until it turns left. Then continue on straight across the field, and across the next one, keeping the steep, grassy drop and the meandering stream on your left.

4 As you come to a field boundary, continue down, keeping this new fence line to your right. At the end of the fence, go over the waymarked stile and turn left. Follow the stream and, at the bottom of the field, go over the waymarked stile. Cross the bridge and go onto the track. Turn left (waymarked) and then right (waymarked) onto the larger track.

5 At the end of the track, turn right and go down the lane. Go over the canal bridge and, if you fancy a break, the Horseshoes Inn is just here. There are some well-preserved lime kilns backing onto the rear garden and, for added interest, benches and tables for outdoor imbibers and relaxers. Lunches and dinners are available daily: 12.00 – 14.30 (15.00 Fri – Sun) and 18.00 – 23.00 (22.30 Sun). This pub is probably the site where horses, once used for towing the canal boats, were changed.

WALK 13

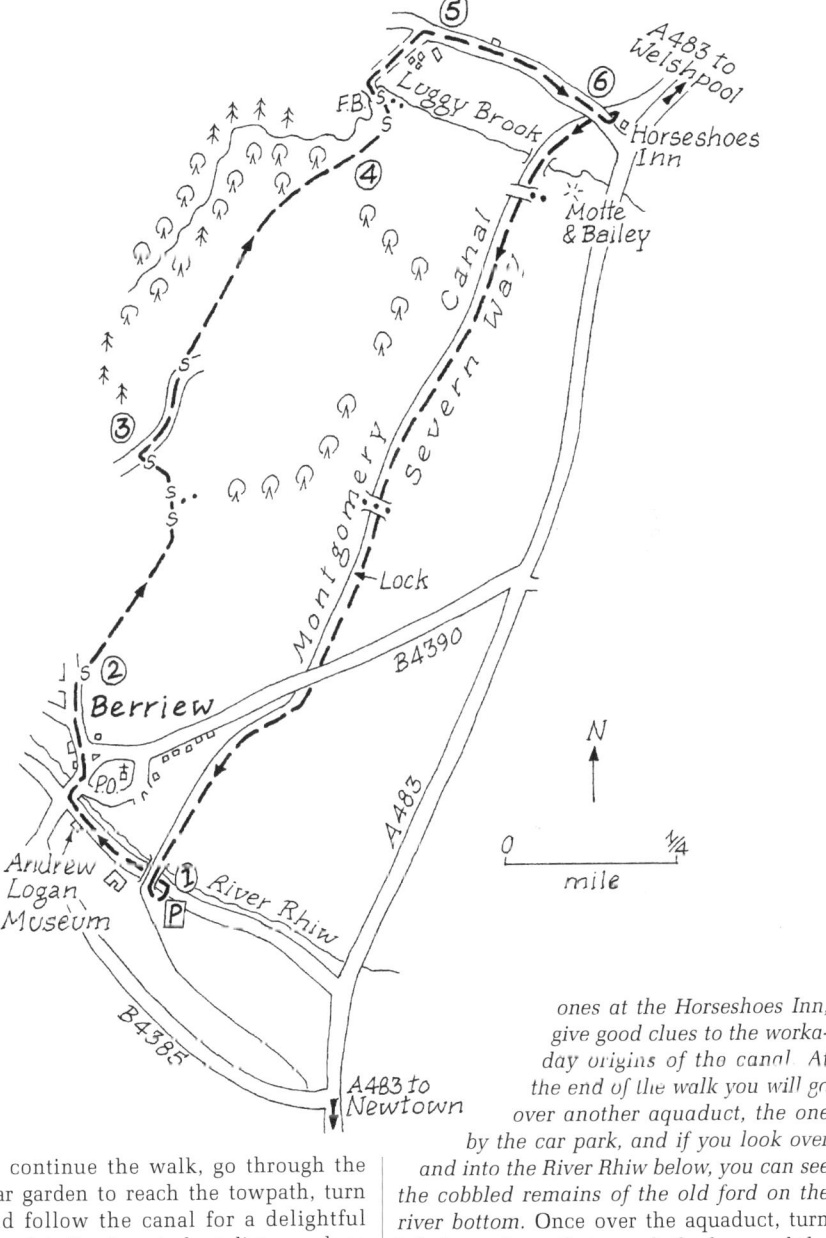

6 To continue the walk, go through the rear garden to reach the towpath, turn left and follow the canal for a delightful amble back to Berriew. A short distance along you will go over an aqueduct, with the canal being carried over the Luggy Brook beneath. After this, look out for the remains of a motte and bailey on the left. You may also spot old wharves and other lime kilns which, with the ones at the Horseshoes Inn, give good clues to the workaday origins of the canal. At the end of the walk you will go over another aqueduct, the one by the car park, and if you look over and into the River Rhiw below, you can see the cobbled remains of the old ford on the river bottom. Once over the aqueduct, turn left down the path to reach the lane and the car park just below.

The village post office sells a booklet on the history of Berriew, should you wish to know more.

WALK 14
LLYN COED Y DINAS NATURE RESERVE
& THE SEVERN VALLEY

DESCRIPTION This walk takes in a peaceful stroll along the River Severn, another pretty stretch of the Montgomery Canal and the opportunity to visit an interesting nature reserve. The walk along the river is beautiful at any time of year, but perhaps especially so on a hot summer's day, when the trees lining the bank are in full leaf and there is always some wildlife to be seen. The canal is often shady, as it is well wooded on both sides for much of the way. It is also a virtually flat walk, making it again ideal for a hot day. Allow around 3 hours for this 5½ mile walk, more if you are visiting the nature reserve. Also connects with **Walk 3. Do not venture near the River Severn if it is in flood.**
START Sarn-y-bryn-caled. Grid Ref: SJ219051.
DIRECTIONS Take the A490 south out of Welshpool. Go for 1¾ miles, until you see the bus shelters on each side of the road. Just after the one on the right, turn right into the lane at Sarn-y-bryn-caled. Please park responsibly here, as it is a residential area. If you are feeling energetic, you can walk along the canal towpath from the Canal Museum or Safeway's car park for about a mile and a quarter, leaving the canal at Belan Locks. Go down Belan Lane and turn left at the houses. You are now at Sarn-y-bryn-caled.

The Llyn Coed Y Dinas Nature Reserve is a perfect example of modern needs dovetailing neatly with the creation of a rich area for wildlife. When the bypass was built in 1994, the gravel needed for the new road was dug out of the fields here. Then, when it was finished, the hole that was left was made into a lake and the surrounding area landscaped to make it suitable for a variety of wildlife habitats, in particular water fowl. The result is a much-needed bypass that has allowed a previously badly congested Welshpool to breathe again, and a new wetland that teems with wildlife. The hide there is roomy and comfortable, with plenty of interesting, child-friendly information placed around its walls, describing the wildlife to be seen, making it a really good venue for a family visit. It's free, has its own car parking area and is open from 09.00 – dusk every day.
Please be very aware that the River Severn has historically been dubbed 'The Wild River' with very good reason. It floods quickly and energetically during prolonged spells of wet weather and even after a single rainstorm, if the general level of the river is high and the ground already soaked. As you go along it is often possible to see the flood level as a visible line of flotsam caught high in the hedges or even spilling over the top. At many places on the route the flood will have been swirling well over your head with strong currents as well, although on a day when the river is contained within its banks it's really very difficult to imagine this. Interestingly, the Severn sometimes shifts its course along the valley, making it difficult to place permanent footpaths along the banks. Anyway, enough of the dangers; for by far the greater part of the year, this is a perfectly safe and enjoyable walk.

1 From Sarn-y-bryn-caled, go back up the lane, cross over the main road near the bus shelter and you will be outside the nature reserve. From here, go on to the roundabout and cross over the bypass on your left (the A483) using the island. Turn into the next road, the continuation of the A490, signposted for Montgomery. Look for a track (not waymarked) immediately after Brandy Cottage, on the right. Go down this track for just over ½ mile, looking for the waymarked post on the left. Go through the gate, across the field and over the stile.

2 This will take you across the runway of Welshpool Airport, where there are notices reminding you to be very careful when crossing. Go over the stile on the other side and walk across the field, keeping left. Go through the gate, keeping the line of willow trees to your right, walk along to the end of this field and take the left field ahead. It is

28

WALK 14

currently unfenced here, though there is a stile. Follow the hedge line, and then head for the river and the left corner of the field as the hedge veers away to the right.

3 At the bridge turn right (waymarked), and follow the line of the river, using the gate and stiles for approximately 2½ miles. For the last bit, the way will take you onto the flood embankment.

4 When you see a farm close to the river on the opposite bank, turn right off the embankment and follow the hedge line, keeping it on your right. Go through the gate ahead and keep the hedge line on your left now, passing the line of sycamores by the boundary of the black and white timbered cottage (Trehelig-gro) that is to your left. Go through the gate ahead.

5 Turn right and follow the track until you reach a crossroads. Go straight ahead if you need to shorten the walk: it will take you straight back to Brandy Cottage. Otherwise, turn left and follow this track to the main road.

6 Cross over onto the footpath, turn left and then right into Belan Lane. Go along until you reach the canal bridge. Just before it, turn right through the gate and down onto the towpath. Turn right and follow the towpath until you reach Belan Locks.

7 Turn right onto the lane and follow it down, turning left at the cottages at the bottom (Sarn-y-bryn-caled). To go to the nature reserve, follow the lane to the bus stop on the main road and cross over here.

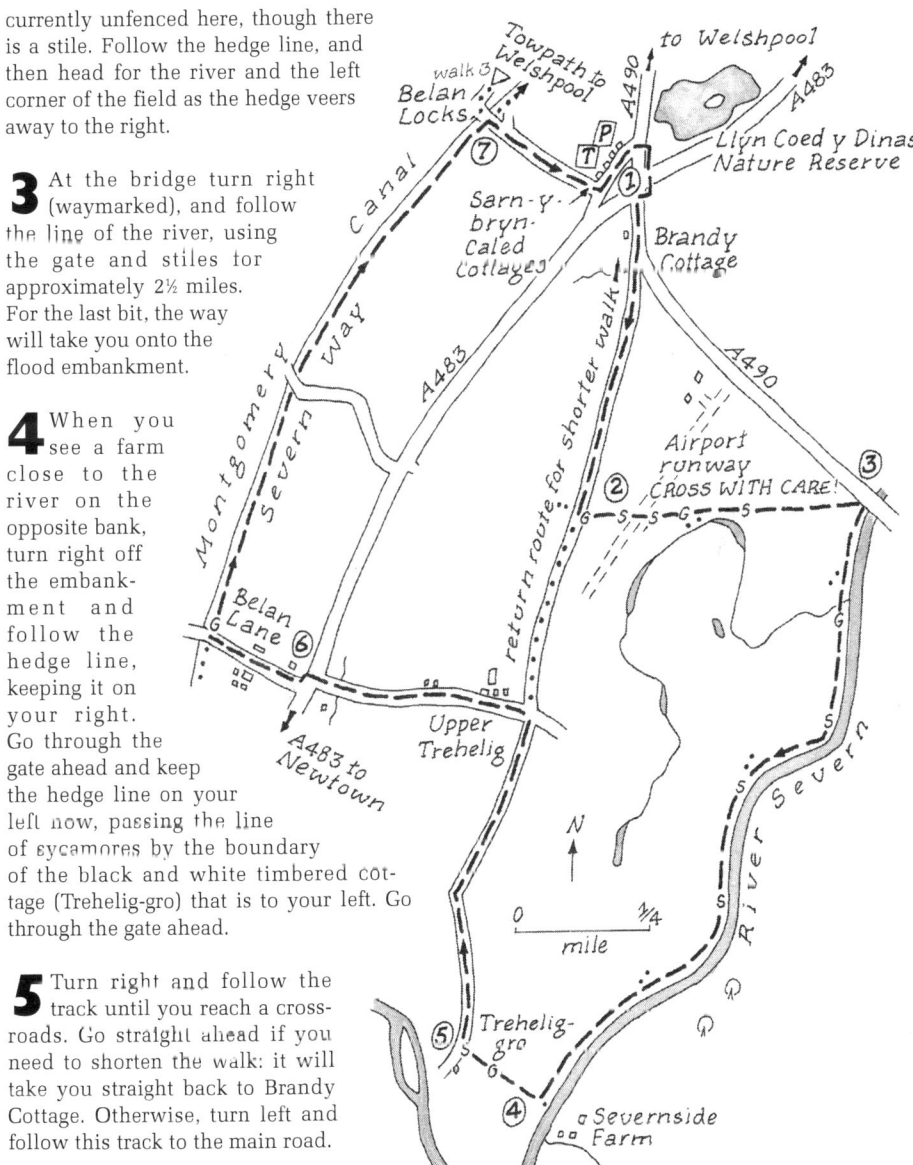

WALK 15
BEACON HILL

DESCRIPTION The last walk in this book takes you quietly through a little bit of history, briefly touching the prehistoric age, the Romans, and through to later times. The walk starts on the ridgeway, takes you down through a green lane and up through farmland to Beacon Hill, where it joins Offa's Dyke Path. It then goes through woodland and quickly down through farmland, giving wide views of the Severn valley and the mountains beyond. From here it is also possible to look over many of the walks in this book. The winding lane then takes you back up to and along the ridgeway, now an ordinary lane though apparently it was once a Roman road. Don't be put off by the comparatively large percentage of lane to be walked on this route, as the two that are used are very quiet and pleasant. Allow around 3 hours for this 6 mile walk.

START The Roman road, near Cwm Dugan, where the telephone wires cross the road. Grid Ref: SJ 263050

DIRECTIONS Take the B4381 east out of Welshpool, crossing over the railway and the bridge over the River Severn. At the junction with the B4388 turn right and go along it for a short distance, taking the first left, signposted for Trelystan and Marton. Follow this lane right up to the top and turn left at the crossroads, signposted for Westbury. Go along this road for ¼ mile, until you see telephone wires crossing the road and the end of the small conifer plantation on your right. On the left is an unmarked track leading to a gate. Park along the road, using the verges ahead. **You will need to park with respect for other road users, keeping clear of the farm and gateways here.** The lane is used for the return route, so it doesn't matter how far along it you park, but do not go beyond the crossroads.

*B*eacon Hill *itself, containing the embanked remains of an ancient hill fort, has reputedly been used through history for the speedy delivery of invasion warnings, and it's easy to see why. Stand at the top and imagine lighting a great bonfire here: the light would be seen well into the panorama of the Welsh mountains before you. Standing on the ridgeway road behind it, and looking to the south-east, there is a clear view across to the Stiperstones and Long Mynd in England. The ridge road is called The Roman Road and they were certainly in the area for a while, as archaeological digs have suggested, though it seems likely that before the Romans it was a prehistoric ridgeway route. If you ignore the verges you can see how very wide the roadway is, indicating a Drover's road. Cattle were driven along here to the Shrewsbury markets and as far as London, until fairly recent times.*

1 Go back to the track now on your right, which is actually a very pretty green lane. Go through the gate and follow it along and down without turning off, passing the small conifer plantation on the left. At the end of this lane, go over the waymarked stile on the right. From here to the lane down on the other side of the hill, the route now follows Offa's Dyke Path. Walk up the field, following the fence line on your left and, *as you go, look for the fine views already appearing behind you.*

2 At the top left hand corner of the field go over the waymarked stile. Go along the track at the edge of the woods and over the next waymarked stile ahead. Walk across this field, keeping the hedge line to your right. *There is now a very attractive panorama, that will keep appearing ever more clearly over the next several miles, showing Welshpool nestling down in the Severn Valley and the broad sweep of mountains behind it. Through the fence on your right are the valleys and hills just over the border in England.* At the top of the field, go over the waymarked stile in the right hand corner, walk uphill, keeping the fence line to your left now, and go over the next waymarked stile tucked into the left hand corner of this field.

3 You are now at the entrance of the ancient Hill Fort which once stood here, the remains of its concentric embankment rings clearly visible. Just ahead is a stone

30

WALK 15

memorial to the planting of this beech woodland in December 1953. The footpath runs round and outside the ring to your left. When you have almost reached the radio mast, go over the stile on your left and follow the path along the edge of the conifer wood, with the fence of the radio mast on your right. The clearly-defined way soon takes you through the trees and is slightly reminiscent of a Grimm's fairy tale path. Going through the latter half of the walk through the woods, waymarked posts will keep you on track. As you are directed out of the wood, look for the waymarked stile ahead, go over and diagonally left across the field, using the Offa's Dyke way-mark post. A waymark post further on down the field shows the way across and up to the far right corner.

4 Go over the waymarked stile and walk down the field, keeping the fence line to your right and crossing into the next field using the waymarked stile. Continue on downhill, still keeping the fence line to your right. At the bottom, go over the waymarke stile. Walk diagonally right down this field to the gate at the bottom right corner. Go over the waymarked stile and go down this field again keeping close to the hedge line on your right. At the bottom, go over the waymarked stile in the right hand corner.

5 Turn right onto the track and follow it until you see a waymark post on your left. Go over it and head down to the next waymarked stile ahead. Since this now stands on its own, the hedge being no longer there, I would say there's no need to climb over it! Go down the next field, look for a similar lonely stile, and head down to the stile at the bottom left corner.

6 Go over and turn right up the lane. Follow this lane uphill to the junction. Turn right and then right again onto the Roman Road (the ridge road). Follow it back to the start.

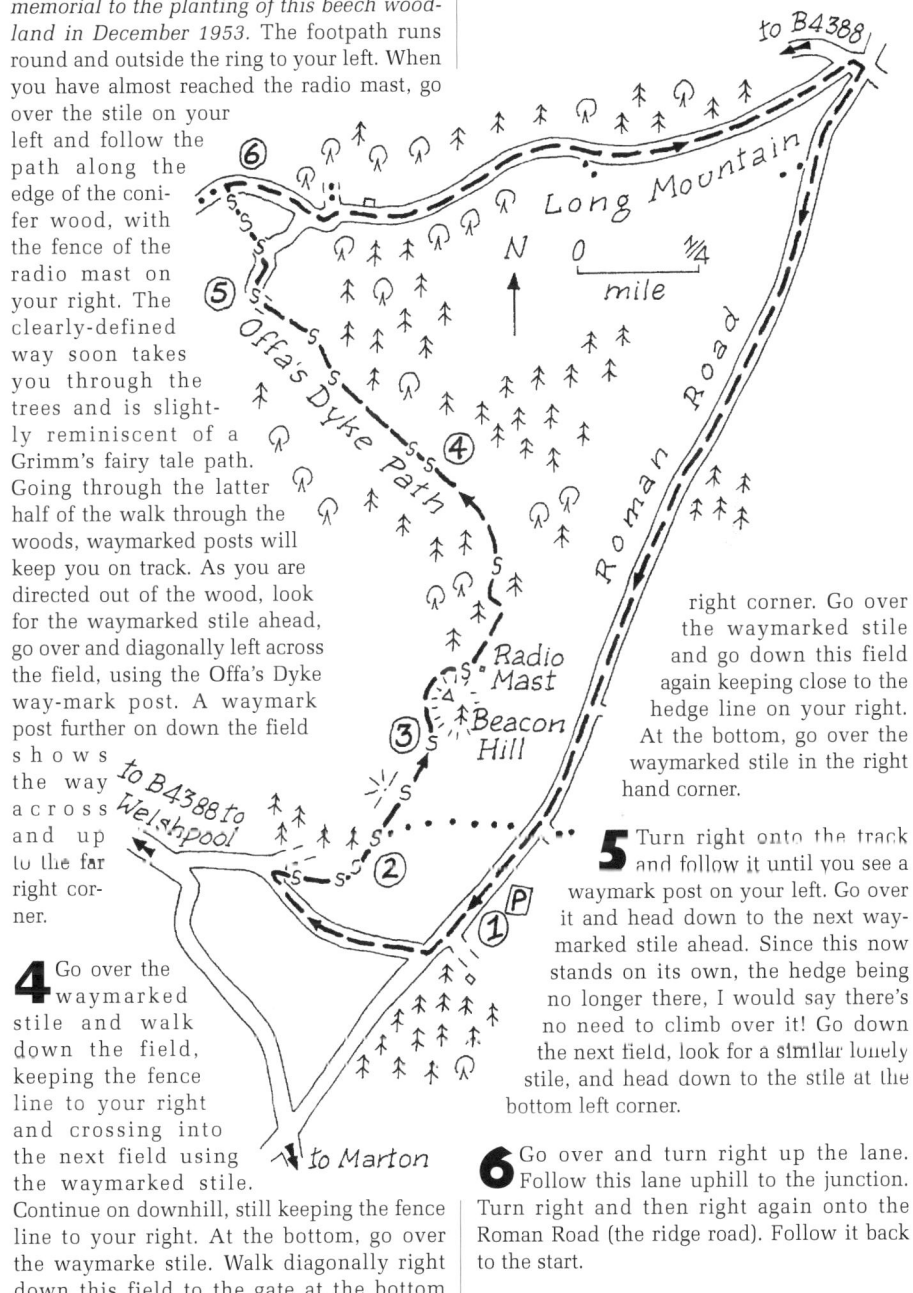

PRONUNCIATION

These basic points should help non-Welsh speakers

Welsh	English equivalent
c	always hard, as in cat
ch	as on the Scottish word lo**ch**
dd	as th in **th**en
f	as f in o**f**
ff	as ff in o**ff**
g	always hard as in **g**ot
ll	no real equivalent. It is like 'th' in then, but with an 'L' sound added to it, giving 'thlan' for the pronunciation of the Welsh 'Llan'.

In Welsh the accent usually falls on the last-but-one syllable of a word.

KEY TO THE MAPS

- → Walk route and direction
- ═ Metalled road
- ─ ─ ─ Unsurfaced road
- •••• Footpath/route adjoining walk route
- ∿ River/stream
- ♣ ♧ Trees
- ▬▬ Railway
- **G** Gate
- **S** Stile
- ☼ Viewpoint
- **P** Parking
- **T** Telephone

THE COUNTRYCODE

Be safe – plan ahead and follow relevant signs

Leave gates and property as you find them

Protect plants and animals, and take your litter home

Keep dogs under close control

Be considerate to other people

Published by
Kittiwake-Books Limited
3 Glantwymyn Village Workshops,
Glantwymyn, Machynlleth, Montgomeryshire
SY20 8LY

© Text: Kirsten Spencer 2003
© Maps & illustrations: Morag Perrott 2003

Cover photos: Main: Breidden Hill – © Wales Tourist Board 2003;
Inset: The Montgomery Canal – David Corbett

Printed by MWL, Pontypool

First edition 2003, reprinted with minor revisions 2005. Reprinted 2008–2012.

ISBN: 978 1 902302 23 2